My First...
Visit to the Dentist

D0306372

First published in the UK in 2009 by
QED Publishing
A Quarto Group Company
226 City Road
London EC1V 2TT
www.qed-publishing.co.uk

A catalogue record for this book is available
from the British Library.

ISBN 978 1 84835 256 8

Author Eve Marleau
Illustrator Michael Garton
Consultants Shirley Bickler and Tracey Dils
Designer Elaine Wilkinson

Publisher Steve Evans
Creative Director Zeta Davies
Managing Editor Amanda Askew

Printed and bound in China

The words in **bold** are
explained in the glossary
on page 24.

My First...
Visit to the Dentist

Eve Marleau and Michael Garton

QED Publishing

Arun and his big brother Nimesh brush their teeth every morning and every night.

Arun likes Nimesh's lovely, bright toothbrush.

It looks just like a space rocket!

"Mum, I'd like a toothbrush just like Nimesh's!"
"Nimesh got his when he went to the dentist."

"When will I go to the dentist?"
"You have an **appointment** with Dr Robinson on Friday."

On Friday, Mum and Arun go to the dentist's **surgery** together. They sit down in the waiting room with the other **patients**.

Jenny has come for a check-up.

Poor Miss Lane the school nurse has a toothache!

"What's wrong with your teeth, Mr Alberti?" asks Arun.

"I have a **cavity**. The dentist needs to fill it before it gets any bigger."

9

"Arun Dutta? Dr Robinson is ready to see you now."

Arun and Mum go into the dentist's office.

In the centre of the room is a big chair,
and a table with some tools on it.

"Come and sit down, Arun,"
Dr Robinson says.

"I'm using a small mirror to count your teeth."

1... 2... 3...
4... 5...
6... 7...

12

"Now I'm checking for cavities."

13

"Finally, I'm scraping any **plaque** from your bottom teeth."

"Plaque is a sticky layer of **bacteria** that can make holes in your teeth if you do not clean them twice a day."

14

Dr Robinson gives Arun a cup of pink mouthwash to rinse his mouth.

"All done!"
says Dr Robinson.

"I'm very pleased, Arun."

"You have strong, healthy teeth and **gums**.
Let me show you how to keep them healthy."

Dr Robinson shows Arun how to clean his teeth.
"Move your brush round and round your teeth."

"Start at the back…

then brush the front…

and make sure
you reach the tops
and the sides."

Dr Robinson shows Arun the posters on the wall.

"Clean your teeth after your breakfast and before you go to bed."

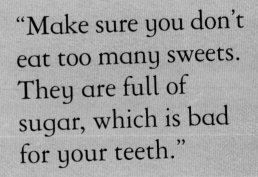

"Make sure you don't eat too many sweets. They are full of sugar, which is bad for your teeth."

"Then your teeth and gums will stay healthy."

"Well done, Arun. You kept your mouth open wide while I checked your teeth," says Dr Robinson.

She opens her drawer, and she brings out a bright-red toothbrush in the shape of a space rocket.

"**Wow!**" says Arun.

"It's just like Nimesh's, but mine is red!"

Now, when he brushes his teeth, Arun makes sure he does just as Dr Robinson said. He moves his brush round and round...

Starting at the back...

then moving to the front...

and finally, he brushes the tops and sides.

His teeth always feel smooth and clean.

They look shiny and white, too!

Glossary

Appointment An arrangement to go somewhere, such as to the dentist, at a certain time.

Bacteria Tiny living cells that can cause tooth decay.

Cavity A hole inside a tooth.

Gums The pink flesh that covers the top of teeth.

Patient A person who is having treatment from the dentist.

Plaque A sticky substance that can form on teeth.

Surgery A place where a dentist gives treatment to the patients.